SCHOLASTIC

create and display

Festivals

Full of exciting activities and displays for the whole curriculum

Ages 5-11
for all primary years

Claire Tinker

SCHOLASTIC

Book End, Range Road, Witney, Oxfordshire, OX29 OYD

www.scholastic.co.uk

1 2 3 4 5 6 7 8 9   0 1 2 3 4 5 6 7 8 9

British Library Cataloguing-in-Publication Data
A catalogue record for this book is available from the British Library.

ISBN 978 -1407-11918 - 2
Printed by Bell & Bain Ltd, Glasgow

Commissioning Editor
Paul Naish

Editor
Janice Baiton

Series Designer and Cover Design
Andrea Lewis

Photography:
RB Photography

Acknowledgements

The author and publisher would like to thank the very talented children at Hunters Bar Junior School for their wonderfully enthusiastic artwork featured in the displays in this book.

Thanks is also due to Headteacher Jill Hallsworth and the staff at Hunters Bar School for their huge support, help and encouragement in the making of this book.

Finally, Claire Tinker would like to thank all her many friends and family who have contributed ideas and information on a huge range of festivals throughout the world.

Contents

Introduction

Religious education in primary school aims to develop children's knowledge and understanding of many different religious beliefs, supporting the values of respect and care for others and preparing young children for a life in a diverse multicultural society. Festivals and special days are a feature of all religions and celebrations, both religious and secular. They occur throughout the world and are an important means of uniting communities, promoting social cohesion and having fun. Some festivals have been around for centuries and others, such as Kwanzaa, are relatively new. Many have deep religious significance while others are secular occasions often based on historical events, such as Bonfire Night. The festivals provided in this book are loosely organised in chronological order and although exact dates have been given wherever possible, many remain flexible – for example, Easter, which always falls on the first Sunday after the first full moon following the spring equinox, can vary by almost a month.

There are quite literally thousands of festivals to choose from and this book is by no means a comprehensive or definitive list of the calendar of festivals the children within your school will celebrate. However, the aim has been to ensure that festivals from most of the world's major religions and cultures are represented as well as smaller lesser-known secularfestivals, such as Up Helly Aa in the Shetland Isles.

Each chapter provides an artistic starting point for teaching festivals in a cross-curricular format. Each festival begins with a brief introduction followed by suggestions on how the children can be encouraged to engage in and understand the special traditions and rituals through art and display. Opportunities for cross-curricular links are provided, particularly in the arts, as music (through the singing of songs), drama and dance are central to many celebrations and festivals. Although there can be quite significant differences within all faith groups throughout the world as to how particular festivals are celebrated, this book aims to provide a starting point for further investigation, discussion and exploration of the many seasonal traditions of festivals that are rich in symbolism, beliefs and ideas and are extremely enjoyable.

Claire Tinker

Kwanzaa (USA)

Kwanzaa is a relatively new festival created in 1966 by Dr Maulana Karenga. It is a week-long African American celebration beginning on 26 December. It is not a religious holiday and does not replace Christmas. It has its origins in the black nationalist movement of the 1960s and aims to bring black people together to celebrate their African roots. Kwanzaa means 'first fruits' in Swahili and is based on the year-end harvest festivals that take place throughout Africa. Seven candles are lit during Kwanzaa, one for every day of the festival. Each day is dedicated to a special theme based on principles intended to strengthen family life and community spirit. These include unity, self-determination, collective, work, creativity and faith. Families decorate their households with traditional craftwork and exchange gifts.

Kwanzaa Designs

Resources

- Pieces of cotton fabric (one per child)
- Fabric dyes
- Black paint and brushes
- Card
- Glue
- Scissors
- Pencils
- Picture of African art and textiles

Approach

1. Show the children some pictures of traditional African art and textiles.
2. Discuss the colours, shapes and motifs.
3. Choose a small pattern or symbol and copy onto a small piece of card in pencil.
4. Cut out the pattern or symbol and stick onto another piece of card. Allow to dry thoroughly.
5. Using fabric dye, paint the cotton fabric in bright colours. Allow to dry.
6. Cover the cardboard symbol in black paint and print a design onto the coloured fabric.

Cross-curricular Links

- **Literacy** – Kwanzaa is a festival that has its roots in the black movement of the 1960s. Study the work of Martin Luther King and his famous speech 'I have a dream'. Challenge the children to write their own version of 'I have a dream' with their own visions of a fairer world.

Christmas (Christianity)

Christmas is a Christian festival that marks the birth of Jesus Christ and is held every year on 25 December in Catholic and Protestant countries. Orthodox Christians in different countries, such as central and eastern Europe, celebrate Christmas on or near 7 January. No one knows the exact date of Jesus' birth but early Christians began to celebrate it around the time of the winter solstice on 21 December. Some Christmas customs come from the Romans who held a festival called Saturnalia during the winter solstice where they exchanged presents and had large banquets.

Many of the customs of Christmas are associated with it taking place during this time. Nowadays Christmas is celebrated in both secular and religious ways with customs linked to many different parts of the world. Nativity plays are performed that tell the story of the birth of Jesus with the visit of the angel Gabriel and the Virgin Mary giving birth to Jesus in a stable. Christmas is also celebrated as a festival of light and is a time for thinking about others less fortunate than ourselves.

Rudolf

Resources

- Papier mâché
- Balloons
- Card
- Collage material
- Cartridge paper for stockings
- Wax pastels

Approach

1. Tell the legend of Saint Nicholas, the fourth-century Bishop of Myra, who is more familiar to the children as Santa Claus. He is often portrayed in a sleigh pulled by reindeers.
   Play the song 'Rudolf the Red-Nosed Reindeer' to the children.
2. Blow up a large balloon and stick papier mâché on it. Allow to dry and attach to a large sheet of card.
3. Decorate as Rudolf and display with brightly coloured paper stockings.

Three Kings

Resources

- Gold spray
- Collage materials
- Glue and scissors
- Versions of the nativity story
- Pictures of the three wise men

Approach

1 Tell the children the story of Christmas. Explain that sometime after Jesus was born three wise men from the East came looking for the child who had been born 'King of the Jews'. The festival of Epiphany celebrates the coming of the Magi (wise men) to Bethlehem with gifts for the infant Jesus (see page 12). There are many different interpretations of the three wise men so show the children various pictures – use the Internet as a resource.

2 Provide a variety of collage material to create a large 3D picture of the three kings. Spray with gold.

Twelve Days of Christmas

Resources

- Copy of the song 'Twelve Days of Christmas' (Dorothy Stott, Schools Specialty Publishing, 2007)
- Cartridge paper
- Gold and green paper
- Wax pastels or paint

Approach

1 Teach the children the song 'Twelve Days of Christmas'. Look at images of the twelve gifts. Discuss ones that might seem unfamiliar to the children, such as four calling birds.

2 Give each child a large number written on a piece of cartridge paper and ask them to decorate it according to the gifts given on that day, for example, five gold rings.

3 Display the numbers with gold paper pears and green paper leaves.

Cross-curricular Links

- **Geography** – The spread of Christianity worldwide means that some people celebrate Christmas in mid-summer. Investigate Christmas in different parts of the world and their different customs and traditions.
- **Maths** – Challenge the children to work out mathematical problems based on the song; for example, how many birds are included in the 12 days of Christmas?

Hanukkah (Judaism)

Hanukkah is a Jewish festival of light held every year on the twenty-fifth day of the Jewish month of Kislev, which can fall anytime from late November to late December. Hanukkah lasts for eight days and commemorates a time more than 2000 years ago when the Jews reclaimed the Temple of Jerusalem after the King of Syria had forbid them to worship there. The Syrians had abused the Jewish temple but it was repaired. The temple's lamp had only enough oil for one day but it stayed alight for eight. This miracle is remembered during the eight days of the festival by lighting a nine-branched candlestick or Menorah. One candle is lit each evening until they all burn together. The ninth candle in the middle is called the Shamash and is used to light the others. There are songs and prayers and people eat special foods such as latkes or potato cakes. Greeting cards are sent and presents are often given, sometimes one for each night of the festival.

Dreidel Game

Resources

- Template of a Dreidel (one per child) (see page 72 for photocopiable resource)
- Coloured crayons or felt pens
- Wooden skewers
- Sellotape®

Approach

1 During Hanukkah, Jewish people play traditional games such as Dreidel. Players spin a four-sided top to win chocolate coins. Ask the children to research the rules of the Dreidel game. Look at designs of a Dreidel and discuss how each side is marked with a Hebrew letter (N, G, H and Sh) which spells out 'A great miracle happened here'.

2 Give the children a template of a Dreidel and decorate accordingly.

3 Demonstrate how to assemble and secure the skewer with Sellotape®.

4 Design and make a board to play the game on.

The Star of David

Resources

- Paper
- Card
- Scissors
- Glue
- Painting equipment
- Fabric
- Art straws

Approach

1 Explain to the children that the Star of David is an important symbol of the Jewish people. The exact origins of the symbol are unknown but it appears on the flag of Israel and dates back centuries. There are many different explanations of the meaning behind the Star of David. One is that the six points of the Star of David are said to symbolise God's rule over the universe in all six directions, which are north, south, east, west, up and down.

2 Demonstrate various processes for painting the Star of David. Allow children a choice of colours and medium to create their own print design based on this Jewish symbol.

3 To make straw designs, sketch out different sized star patterns on a sheet of paper, measure and cut art straws to cover the design.

Cross-curricular Links

- **Maths** – The Dreidel game is a game of chance. Discuss chance and probability in maths and design new games.
  The Star of David is made up of two large triangles. Point out the two triangles and discuss how they overlap to form other smaller triangles. Count the number of triangles it creates. Are there any other shapes created? For example, hexagon. Experiment with different ways of overlapping triangles to make patterns and shapes.

Hogmanay (Scotland)

Hogmanay is the Scottish word for the celebration that welcomes in the New Year. Historians believe that the celebration was inherited from the Vikings who, coming from an even more northerly country than Scotland, eagerly looked forward to the arrival of the winter solstice (shortest day) and celebrated its passing.

In the past, Christmas was not celebrated as a festival in Scotland and for many years from the end of the seventeenth century it was virtually banned for religious reasons. As late as the 1950s, Hogmanay was the major Scottish festival of the winter season as many people worked during the Christmas holiday.

There are numerous traditions and customs associated with Hogmanay. Immediately after the bells have chimed at midnight people link arms and sing Robert Burns' (1759–1796) 'For Auld Lang Syne'. On the last stroke of midnight a man is invited into the house bringing a lump of coal, bread and a coin. The gifts are symbolic of good wishes for warmth, food and wealth for the coming year and the custom is called 'first footing', meaning the first foot in the house after midnight. Traditionally the first foot should be a dark-haired man, a custom that probably goes back to the days when a blond-haired stranger could be a Viking and consequently not particularly welcome!

Hogmanay Bells

Resources

- Balloons
- Cellulose paste powder and water
- Scrap paper
- Card and glue
- Paints and paintbrushes
- Paper and sequins for the 2D bells

Approach

1. Blow up balloons and cover the top half with papier mâché.
2. When dry, pop the balloon and trim the papier mâché into the shape of a bell.
3. Attach the bell to a large sheet of card with PVA glue.
4. Use gold paint and sequins to decorate the bells.
5. To make the 2D paper bells, cut out a template and provide the children with colour paint, sequins etc. Draw a pattern on the paper and then paint and decorate.

Tartan

Resources

- Examples of tartan designs
- Paint and paintbrushes
- Coloured art straws
- Glue and scissors
- Cartridge paper

Approach

1. Show the children pictures of Scottish tartan. Tartan has become one of the main symbols of Scotland and Scottish culture, and although it is often worn in the form of a kilt at special occasions, it can be part of normal daywear for Scottish people. Explain that it is a woven material, generally made of wool with strips of different colours. The arrangement of the strips can be in many different combinations of colours and vary in depth.
2. Give the children the opportunity to experiment with designs and colour combinations.
3. When the children have a composition they are happy with, ask them to transfer their design onto a piece of cartridge paper.
4. Paint and add art straws to enhance the overall design.

Cross-curricular Links

- **Science** – In science, study the time zones of the world. Work out when different cities celebrate New Year and Hogmanay.
- **Music** – Listen to some traditional Scottish bagpipe music. Discuss how bagpipes work by storing air in the bag and squeezing it out to make the reeds in the various tubes play.
- **Dance** – Scottish Highland dancing is one of the oldest forms of folk dance. Watch videos of people performing the Highland fling, a dance carried out originally at the end of a victorious battle. Practise dancing the Highland fling to the sound of bagpipe music.

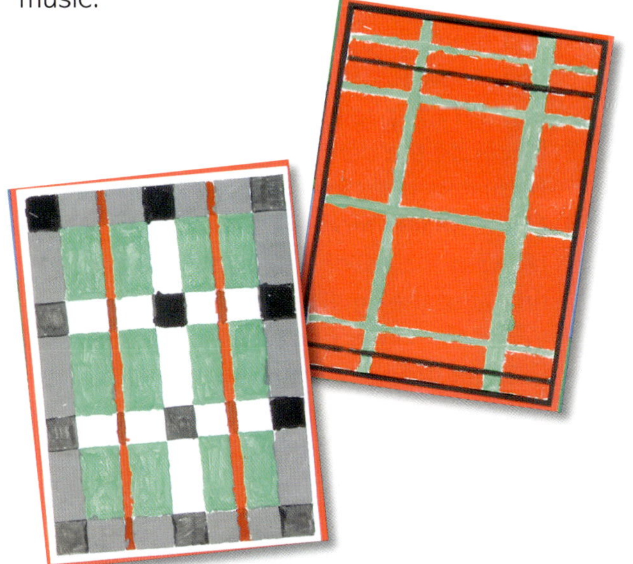

Epiphany (Christianity)

The Christian festival of Epiphany (or Twelfth Night) on 6 January marks the end of the 12 days of Christmas and is traditionally the day when all Christmas decorations are taken down. The term 'epiphany' means 'to show' or 'to reveal'. Epiphany is the day in the Christmas calendar when Christians remember the coming of the wise men bringing gifts of gold, frankincense and myrrh to the Christ child. By bringing these gifts, the wise men 'reveal' Jesus to the world as lord and king.

In Russia there is a character in folklore called Babushka who is said to have looked after the three wise men on their journey to Bethlehem. They asked Babushka to join their quest but she explained that her housework was not yet finished, so they bid her farewell and went on their way. However, she soon changed her mind, gathered some gifts for the baby and went in search of the three wise men. Legend has it that ever since she has been searching for the Christ child and on Epiphany eve she leaves presents in each home of the people she visits in the hope they too will search for the child.

3D Babushka

Resources

- A version of the Babushka story (e.g. *Babushka* by Arthur Scholey (author) and Helen Cann (illustrator), Candlewick Press)
- Pictures of a Babushka doll
- Paint and paintbrushes
- Balloons
- Papier mâché

Approach

1 Read the story of Babushka and show the children pictures of Babushka dolls. Discuss the patterns and colours used.
2 Cover an inflated balloon with papier mâché and mould into the shape of a Babushka doll. Allow to dry, pop the balloon inside and cut the papier mâché shape in half.
3 Decorate the doll using the picture of Babushka dolls for inspiration.
4 Make smaller models in the same way by blowing the balloon up slightly less each time. Put the smaller decorated balloons inside the larger ones to recreate Babushka Russian dolls.

2D Babushka Dolls

Resources

- A version of the Babushka story
- Pictures of Babushka Russian dolls
- Paint and paintbrushes
- Cartridge paper template of a Babushka doll

Approach

1 Read the story of Babushka and show the children pictures of Babushka dolls. Discuss the patterns and colours used. Babushka dolls or Russian nested dolls are a set of dolls of decreasing size, which fit inside one another, the set of dolls range from 5 to 30. The first doll was made by a Russian craftsman in a toy workshop in 1890 and consisted of eight dolls.

2 Give each child a copy of a Babushka doll template and ask the children to design their own Babushka doll.

3 Traditionally the outer layer of a Babushka doll is a woman dressed in a long pinafore dress known as a sarafan and holding a rooster.

Cross-curricular Links

- **Design and Technology** – In England, people used to have parties on Twelfth Night and celebrate with a cake. The cake was a rich fruitcake and often had a dried bean and a dried pea hidden inside. If you found the bean or pea you were crowned Twelfth Night king or queen. Find a recipe and make a Twelfth Night cake.
- **Literacy** – Twelfth Night was a traditional time for 'mummings', which are a type of folk play that combine music, dance and sword fighting performed most commonly in England. The players known as 'mummers' were amateurs and all male. It is thought that William Shakespeare named his comedy *Twelfth Night* as it was first performed as part of *Twelfth Night* celebrations in 1601. Read the Shakespeare play *Twelfth Night*. There are many adaptions of his plays written especially for young people, such as *Mr William Shakespeare's Plays* by Marcia Williams (Walker Books).

Tu B'Shevat (Judaism)

Jewish people herald the coming of spring with a festival called Tu B'Shevat. It marks the end of winter and means the fifteenth (tu) day of Shevat (the eleventh month of the Jewish calendar). This is usually sometime in late January or early February. Jewish children throughout the world take part in tree planting ceremonies. Long ago a cedar tree was planted for every baby boy born and a cypress tree for every girl.

Jewish people living outside of Israel celebrate the festival by eating fruit, particularly the kinds grown there, such as pomegranates, grapes, figs, olives and dates. The Torah (the first part of the Jewish Bible) praises seven 'fruits' in particular wheat, barley, grapes, figs, pomegranates, olives and dates. It is also the custom to eat a new fruit, one that has not been eaten that year and a short blessing is recited.

Blossom Tree

Resources

- Photocopies of a winter tree (one per child)
- Matchsticks
- Paint

Approach

1 Explain to the children that this festival celebrates the importance of trees to the Jewish nation to mark the end of winter and Jewish children plant trees to symbolise a 'New Year of trees'.
2 Talk about other customs during the festival of Tu B'Shevat.
3 Give the children a photocopy of a winter tree and demonstrate that by using a matchstick dipped in different shades of pink and green it can be transformed into a spring tree full of blossom.
4 To create the display, enlarge the picture of the tree either by photocopying it in sections or by asking the children to paint a large version and display their trees around it.

Observational Fruits

Resources

- Real-life fruits
- Photographs of the fruit
- Drawing pencils
- Cartridge paper
- Pastels

Approach

1 Explain that Jewish people eat lots of fruit on Tu B'Shevat, not only the ones associated with Israel (grapes, figs, pomegranates) but also some they may not have tasted before.
2 Bring a collection of fruits (in this case, pineapple). Make a still life display and encourage the children to observe carefully the shapes and texture of the fruit.
3 Using a variety of mixed media, draw the fruit and make a class collage of everyone's drawings.
4 Create the large pineapple display by cutting up photographs of a pineapple and make a photo montage.

Cross-curricular Links

- **Geography** – During Tu B'Shevat, families support reforestation projects in Israel. Look at the importance of trees in controlling our climate etc. Discuss reforestation projects around the world and the impact on our environment.
- **Design and Technology/Science** – Make a collection of different fruits and give the children the opportunity to observe the various shapes, colours, textures, smells etc. Encourage the children to taste the fruits, especially ones they haven't eaten before. Make charts of favourite fruits. Discuss the health benefits of 'five a day'.
  N.B. Be aware of the risks of food allergies.

Up Helly Aa (Scotland)

Up Helly Aa is a Scottish festival from the Shetland Islands held on the last Tuesday of January. The festival takes place at night when a 10 metre Viking galley leads a torchlight procession through the streets of Lerwick. Blazing torches are carried by brilliantly dressed guizers, who usually make their own costumes in strict secrecy. Only the chief guizer leads the procession and his squad dress up as Vikings. The galley is mounted on wheels and has a dragon's head and two rows of heraldic shields.

The climax of the procession is when the torches are thrown into the galley. On the smaller islands, the galley is then pushed out to sea, but in Lerwick it is burnt in the centre of the town. The guizers have three songs, the 'Up Helly Aa Song' (which is sung as the procession starts off), the 'Galley Song' (which is sung before the torches are thrown into the galley) and 'The Norseman's Home' (which is sung when the galley is burning). It is a friendly, family event where the whole community takes part with the children dressing up as Vikings.

Viking Galley

Resources

- Pictures of Viking boats and shields
- Circular pieces of card
- Strips of balsa wood
- Black, yellow, red paint
- Brushes
- Foil mirrors

Approach

1 Give each child examples of Viking shields. Study the designs, colour etc.

2 Ask the children to recreate a Viking shield using typical designs and colours. Provide children with a circular piece of card and ask them to sketch out a suitable design. Paint and when dry, cut half way into the shield and make the shield slightly 3D by folding and stapling it together. Stick a foil mirror in the middle.

3 Provide the children with a large piece of card and ask them to sketch out a design of a Viking galley. Cover in balsa wood and decorate with a sail and mini versions of their shields.

4 Display the shields around the Viking galley.

Fair Isle Bobble Hat

Resources

- Squared paper
- Examples of Fair Isle knitting patterns
- Coloured crayons
- Wool pom-poms or card and wool

Approach

1 Fair Isle is the southern-most island of the Shetland Isles and is the home to the Shetland sheep, which produce hard-wearing fleeces that provide the wool for the local knitting tradition. Explain to the children that Fair Isle knitting is a distinctive style associated with the Shetland Isles. It consists of horizontal bands of symmetrical patterns.

2 Give the children a piece of squared paper and show them examples of Fair Isle patterns.

3 Using coloured crayons, challenge the children to create a group (four or six children's contributions) bobble hat.

4 Display hats with wool pom-poms.

Cross-curricular Links

- **History** – Study the Viking invasion and the reasons for Vikings settling in the Shetland Isles. Investigate their way of life and make factfiles.
- **Music** – The 'Up Helly Aa' song was originally sung to the tune of 'John Brown's Body' until 1921 when Mr Thomas Manson composed the tune with which it has since been associated. Write new verses for the song.
- **Geography** – Study the climate, vegetation and wildlife of the Shetland Isles.

Chinese New Year (Worldwide)

The date of the Chinese New Year changes from year to year because it follows an ancient farming calendar and can fall anytime between late January and the middle of February. It lasts for 15 days and is the most important Chinese festival. Each Chinese New Year is named after one of 12 animals, each of which has its own personality.

The story tells how all the animals took part in a race to decide which one should start the cycle of the years. The race involved crossing a river and despite all the animals starting together, ox soon has a clear lead. While all the other animals were struggling behind, rat jumped onto ox's back and was carried across the river. Just before ox reached the other side of the river rat leapt onto the bank and won the race, followed by the ox, the tiger, the hare (or rabbit), the dragon, the snake, the horse, the ram (or sheep), the monkey, the rooster, the dog and the pig. The origins of this festival are religious (Taoism) but much of the present-day celebration is secular and includes spectacular parades with dragon and lion dancers.

Chinese Fans

Resources

- Commercially brought plain fans
- Collection of materials to make own fans – silk, silk paints, paint, paint brushes, paper
- Pictures of Chinese New Year art

Approach

1. Tell the story of the Chinese New Year. Give the children pictures of Chinese New Year art to study and ask them to make some preliminary designs that can be transferred onto a fan.
2. Allow the children time to explore all the different materials and make a choice of how they are going to make and decorate their fan. If necessary demonstrate various techniques.
3. When dry display the fans in a circular design.

Chinese Lanterns

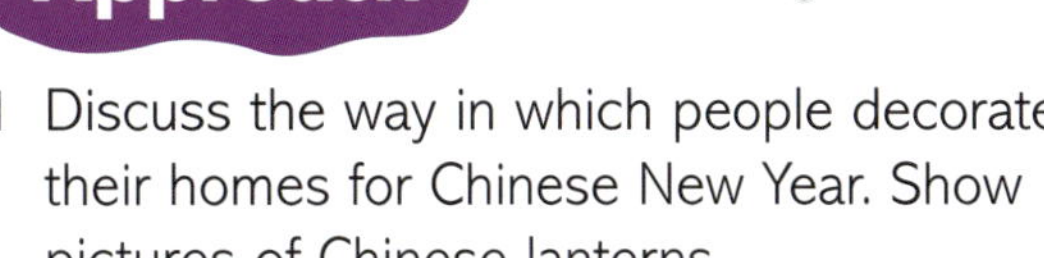

Approach

1 Discuss the way in which people decorate their homes for Chinese New Year. Show pictures of Chinese lanterns.
2 To make Chinese lanterns, attach withy canes together with masking tape to make the frame. Mix PVA glue and water in a bowl and use a sponge to carefully cover a sheet of tissue paper with glue. Drape the tissue paper over the withy cane frame and cover with another layer of PVA mixture so that the tissue dries hard.
3 Embellish with collage materials.

Cross-curricular Links

- **Literacy** – In drama, act out the story of the Chinese New Year. Write the Chinese New Year story from various animals' points of view. Read *The Firework Maker's Daughter* by Philip Pullman.
- **Maths** – Invent and solve mathematical problems using Chinese numbers.

Resources

- Pictures of Chinese lanterns
- Commercially brought plain Chinese lanterns
- Withy canes (long, bendable willow sticks) and masking tape
- PVA glue and sponges
- Gold and red tissue paper
- Collage materials to embellish design

Venice Carnival (Italy)

The Venice Carnival starts ten days before Shrove Tuesday and finishes on the stroke of midnight on this day. The origins of the carnival go back to around 1162 CE to celebrate a battle victory. The Republic defeated Ulrico, Patriarch of Aquileia and a tradition of slaughtering a bull and 12 pigs in Piazza San Marco originated to commemorate the victory.

However, it took another 134 years before the city senate declared the celebrations official and over the years it has gathered momentum and become an internationally known festival. It is famous for its flamboyant costumes and carnival masks. Each year the carnival establishes a theme, for instance in 2010 the theme was 'Sensation – six senses for six neighbourhoods'. The two-week festival includes a series of processions, masquerades, music and theatre.

Venetian Mask Display

Resources

- Pictures of Venice Carnival
- Plastic masks (or papier mâché balloons cut in half)
- Examples of Venetian masks
- Pictures of the carnival
- Collage materials
- Paint and brushes
- Glue
- Cartridge paper
- Card

Approach

1 Explain to the children that masks have always been a feature of the Venice Carnival. Look at pictures of the carnival and, if possible, at some actual Venetian masks. They can be made in leather or papier mâché, hand painted and embellished with feathers, sequins and gems.

2 Give the children examples of Venetian masks to study and ask them to sketch out their own ideas for a mask.

3 Demonstrate how to transfer ideas from their design sheets to the mask using poster paint.

4 Give each child a plastic mask or they can prepare their own by covering a balloon with papier mâché (dried and cut in half). Ask the children to transfer their ideas onto the three-dimensional shape.

5 Stick the mask or half balloon onto a sheet of card and allow to dry.

6 Embellish masks with feathers, sequins etc.

7 Display the masks with 2D carnival balloons made from cartridge paper.

3D Venetian Mask

Resources

- Papier mâché
- Balloon
- Cardboard
- Collage material – felt, net, feathers
- Glue, scissors
- Paint, paint brushes
- Plastic mask

Approach

1 Blow up a balloon and cover with papier mâché.
2 Allow to dry and, using cardboard, create a secure base to support the papier mâché balloon.
3 Glue a plastic mask onto the balloon and allow to dry.
4 Sketch out a design of a carnival mask. If required, give the children a particular theme, such as 'winter'.
5 Use paint to create a base for the decoration of the mask.
6 Transfer the design using various collage materials.

Cross-curricular Links

- **Geography** – Research the city of Venice and the country of Italy. Make a factfile of the country's climate and notable landmarks.
- **Music** – The 'Carnival of Venice' song by Jean-Baptiste Arban is a famous piece inspired by the carnival of Venice. It is an Italian folk song that many great cornet players have performed. Listen to the various versions of the song and try to identify the different musical instruments.

Animex (England)

The Animex International Festival of Animation and Computer Games takes place in Middlesbrough in the north of England at the start of February. It began as a two-day series of lectures by animators at the University of Teesside in February 2000 and has since grown into a yearly week-long festival that provides animators, directors, students, artists, designers, writers and educators with a platform to celebrate and promote the art of animation. The festival provides workshops in many aspects of creative visualisation, including character animation, sculpting for animation, character development and design, and animation writing.

Animation is the rapid display of a sequence of images to create an illusion of movement. It is an optical illusion, a trick of the human eye called persistence of vision. There are many different ways of making pictures move and the phenakistoscope, thaumatrope and zoetrope were all early popular animation devices. These can be made and used easily by children. With the development of the motion camera and projector, animations become more sophisticated. Walt Disney (1901–1966), perhaps the most famous animator in history, created his first Mickey Mouse cartoon in 1928.

Disney Characters

Resources

- Examples of Disney or cartoon animation
- Paint and brushes
- Cartridge paper

Approach

1 Explain to the children that in 1937 Walt Disney Studios released *Snow White and the Seven Dwarfs* and it was the first fully animated feature film in history. It pioneered a new medium in film and entertainment.

2 Give the children examples of cartoon animation characters, ask them to choose their favourite and to draw and paint pictures of them. Alternatively, they could create their own animation characters.

Zoetrope

The zoetrope is an optical toy in the form of a cylinder with slits in the sides. When a strip of pictures is placed on its inner surface and the cylinder is rotated, the pictures appear to come to life.

Resources

- Commercially brought zoetrope
- Strips of paper
- Crayons

Approach

1. Explain the concept of persistence of vision and demonstrate how this works by spinning a strip of sequenced drawings in the zoetrope and showing how the pictures blur together producing the illusion of motion.
2. Give the children a strip of paper separated into blank sections.
3. Demonstrate how to draw a sequence of pictures, each one being slightly different to the previous one.
4. Put the strip inside the drum and spin.

Cross-curricular Links

- **Science** – Explore the concept of persistence of vision, a principle first recognised by a Greek mathematician called Euclid. Experiment with other ways of making pictures move, such as flipbooks, phenakistoscope and thaumatropes.
- **Literacy** – The process of creating an animation story on film is very structured. Study the process and ask the children to create storyboards, dialogue for characters etc, leading to a full-screen script for an animation character.
- **Design and Technology** – Set the children the challenge of making their own zoetrope. Provide suitable materials and evaluate the effectiveness of the children's designs.

Argungu (Nigeria)

Argungu is a four-day fishing festival held in northern Nigeria every February or March. It began in 1934 to mark the end of a century of hostility between the Sokoto Caliphate and the Kebbi Kingdom. Some people celebrate by wearing clothes with fish patterns on them. On the final day of the festival there is a fishing competition. At the sound of a gunshot thousands of men and boys wade into the river and have one hour to catch the largest fish. They carry nets and big gourds called calabashes and drive large fish called Nile perch into the shallow water where they can be caught. The man who catches the largest fish receives a prize.

T-Shirt Designs

Resources

- Examples of tessellating fish patterns by Maurits Cornelis Escher
- Squared paper
- Cartridge paper
- Paint and brushes

Approach

1. Talk about what happens during the Argungu festival. Explain to the children how some people dress up in clothes with fish patterns on them.
2. Show examples of fish tessellating patterns by M.C. Escher (1898–1972). Using squared paper, demonstrate how to create a tessellating tile that could be made to look like a fish.
3. Allow the children time to experiment before giving out a piece of cartridge paper shaped as a T-shirt to transfer their design onto.
4. Display with paintings of fish.

Fish Collage

Resources

- Large sheet of card
- Glue
- Pencils
- Shells
- Pictures of fish

Approach

1 Show the children various pictures of fish. Discuss the shapes and colours.
2 Arrange children to work in groups. Give each group a large sheet of card and ask the children to sketch a large picture of a fish.
3 Provide a variety of shells and encourage the children to sort them into colours and sizes and stick them onto the collage.

Cross-curricular Links

- **Design and Technology** – Discuss the value of fish in a healthy diet. Look at recipes that use different types of fish and write own recipe.
- **Literacy** – Write poems about fish. Use different techniques, such as alliteration and repetition, to create the feeling of fish moving.
- **Geography** – Research the country of Nigeria. It is one of Africa's leading oil producers. Discuss other exports of the country.
- **History** – Nigeria is a former British colony. Research what this means.

Hina Matsuri (Japan)

Hina Matsuri is a Japanese festival that takes place every year on 3 March. It is often called the Japanese doll festival. The Japanese believe that a person's illness or bad luck can be passed on to dolls. Families who are worried about the health of their children donate dolls in a special ceremony at a Shinto shrine where special prayers are said before the dolls are piled high on a board and sent out to sea. It is hoped that as they float away they would take the illnesses and bad luck with them. For this reason the dolls are often called 'casting off dolls'. On 3 March, girls dress up in a traditional kimono and show their beautiful dolls to friends at parties.

Kimono Designs

The kimono is the traditional national dress of Japan. Today kimonos are most often worn by women and for special occasions only. The designs on kimonos are created using many different techniques including appliqué batik and weaving. The patterns often complement the seasons with bright colours and floral patterns in the spring and richer colours and patterns in the autumn.

Resources

- Pictures of Japanese patterns, imagery, kimonos
- Cartridge paper, cut into squares
- Viewfinders
- Paint and brushes

Approach

1 If possible, bring a kimono into the classroom to show the children. Discuss the imagery used in a traditional kimono, such as peonies, cherry blossom, chrysanthemums and maple leaves. Try to identify these flowers on either real kimonos or pictures of kimonos.

2 Encourage the children to use a viewfinder to highlight areas of interest on Japanese designs. Sketch out possible kimono designs.

3 Transfer designs onto square sheets of cartridge paper and then paint them.

Origami Dolls

Origami is the Japanese art of paper folding. 'Ori' is the Japanese word for folding and 'kami' means paper. Origami is always made using a squared piece of paper and there are many different ways of folding the square to create a doll shape.

Resources

- Examples of origami-folded doll designs
- Scrap squared paper
- Origami paper

Approach

1 Look at various origami-folding designs (e.g. www.tammyyee.com/printempress.html or www.enchantedlearning.com/crafts/origami/doll/). Investigate different folding shapes that can be made into a doll picture. Encourage the children to design their own folding origami designs.
2 When the children have a design they are happy with, either their own or a published example, practise the folds on scrap paper before using origami paper to create the dolls.
3 Add faces to the dolls and display as a group origami collage.

Cross-curricular Links

- **ICT** – Use the Internet to find out about Japanese Boys' Day on 5 May called Kodomo-no-hi.

Mothering Sunday (Christianity)

Mothering Sunday is always held on the fourth Sunday of Lent and as such will always alter according to when Easter falls. Centuries ago it was the custom for people to return to the church where they were baptised for a special service on the fourth Sunday of Lent. Although it is not certain how the idea of Mothering Sunday started, it is thought that the origins began with the tradition of returning to the 'Mother Church' in Lent. In Victorian times it became a day when children were given the day off from work as domestic servants or apprentices to visit their mother. They would take gifts of flowers or Simnel cakes. Today it is a day when children pay respect to their mothers and give gifts and flowers.

Flower Patterns

Resources

- Stencil of a flower
- Sheets of cartridge paper
- Wax pastels

Approach

1. Talk to the children about the origins of Mothering Sunday. The role of the mother may be a sensitive issue for some children. There are many different family structures where different people fulfil the role of 'mother' and some thoughtfulness needs to be employed. Talk about different ways of saying thank you and showing appreciation to the people that care for us.
2. Give the children a flower template and demonstrate how to draw round it to create interesting shapes and patterns. Alternatively, the children could create their own templates.
3. Allow the children to experiment with designs before choosing their favourite. Fill in designs using brightly coloured pastels.

Quilling Card

Quilling is the art of rolling and shaping thin strips of paper to form a picture. Bought quilling strips can be used or paper strips can be made easily in different thicknesses depending on the age and dexterity of the children doing the project.

Resources

- Commercially bought or hand-made quilling strips
- Pencils or matchsticks
- PVA glue
- Sheet of card (one per child)

Approach

1. Fold a sheet of card in half.
2. Demonstrate how to roll the strips around a pencil or matchstick, glue the strip at the end and remove to create a quilling roll. Show the children how to pinch the scrolls to make different shapes.
3. When the children have made several scrolls, show them how to arrange the scrolls to make quilling flowers. Attach using PVA glue.

Cross-curricular Links

- **PSHCE** – In addition to Mother's Day, Father's Day is celebrated in June. Talk to the children about people who care for us in different ways and at different times, such as stepmothers, foster mothers, extended families etc. Make a class poster of all the different people who contribute to the care of the class community.
- **History** – Research the history of child labour in Victorian times and the working conditions.

Holi (Hinduism)

Holi is a Hindu spring festival often called the 'Festival of colours'. It takes place over two days in February or March. Although Holi has religious roots, it primarily marks the arrival of spring and is a festival of fun. There are several legends associated with Holi. A particular one is that long ago there was an evil king named Hiranyakashipu. He had a son called prince Prahlad who often worshiped Lord Vishnu. This infuriated his father who tried to kill his son. Several attempts failed and he finally ordered his sister Holika to enter a blazing fire with Prahlad on her lap.

The demon Holika was meant to be immune to fire but she was unaware that this was only if she entered the fire alone. Holika was burnt to death and Prahlad was safe. The legend goes that before Holika died she begged for forgiveness. Prahlad granted her wishes and said her name would be remembered once a year and so the festival of Holi was celebrated. The celebration is to symbolise good overcoming evil.

Hand Display

Resources

- Story of Holi
- Paint and brushes
- Wax pastels
- Template of hand
- Cartridge paper

Approach

1. Introduce the children to the story of Holi. Explain that as part of the celebrations of the festival, people throw coloured powder or water at others.
2. Give the children a choice of medium to create their patterned coloured hand. Provide a large template of a hand for them to draw around, cut out and decorate.
3. Display the hands on a brightly coloured background with large paper hands decorated with splashes of paint.

Peacock Display

The peacock is the national bird of India and is fully protected under the Indian Wildlife Protection Act 1972. It is prominent in legends and folklore of the Indian people. Peacocks always accompany the image of Lord Krishna and a peacock feather forms part of his crown. The festival of Holi is closely connected with Lord Krishna (an incarnation of Vishnu) and his love for Radha. Many legends revolve around him, and the young Lord Krishna has often been portrayed as a mischievous prankster who loved playing jokes. It is said that he started the trend of throwing colours after he applied colour to the face of his beloved Radha to make her more like him.

Resources

- Strips of black card
- Wax pastels
- Peacock feathers
- Felt
- Sequins and card to make the peacock

Approach

1 Show the children the peacock feathers and discuss the significance of the peacock in Indian folklore.
2 Encourage the children to look closely at the colours and using wax pastels, draw the feather on black card.
3 Display the individual drawings as a fanned peacock with felt feathers and a sequined peacock in the foreground.

Cross-curricular Links

- **RE** – At the same time as Hindus celebrate Holi, many Sikhs hold their own festival called Hola Mohalla. Investigate the similarities and differences of the two festivals.
- **Literacy** – Write a play script for the story of Holi and act it out. Make props and costumes.

Easter (Christianity)

Easter is the most important festival of the Christian year. At Easter, Christians are reminded of the crucifixion of Jesus Christ and his resurrection on Easter day. Easter always falls on the first Sunday after the first full moon following the spring equinox (21 March). The equinox occurs when the day and the night are of equal length. The festival cannot fall earlier than 22 March or later than 25 April. Easter is a festival for hope and renewed life and there are many customs associated with it. Eggs are often given as gifts as they represent new life. The custom of giving chocolate eggs was a twentieth-century invention. In certain countries it is the custom to hollow out eggshells and paint them in colourful patterns.

Easter Chicks

Resources

- Cartridge paper
- Scissors and glue
- Wax pastels
- Collage materials, e.g. feathers

Approach

1. Fold a sheet of white paper in half. Make a 2–3 cm cut through the fold. Fold the flaps outwards at an angle then push them inwards again.
2. Open the paper and pull the flaps out to form the chick's beak. Draw the outline of a chick's head around the beak and attach a backing sheet.
3. Colour and decorate the chick.
4. Display the chicks in and around some collaged eggs.

3D Easter Eggs

Easter eggs are given as gifts to celebrate the festival of Easter and are a symbol of new life, rebirth and springtime. Originally these were dyed or painted chicken eggs and the custom of giving chocolate eggs is relatively modern with the first mass-produced chocolate egg appearing around 1873. In the past, people would create papier mâché eggs and put small gifts inside. The most famous decorated eggs were made by Peter Carl Fabergé (1846–1920), a well-known goldsmith. He made his first egg in 1885, which was commissioned by Tsar Alexander III of Russia as a surprise gift for his wife.

Resources

- Pictures of Fabergé eggs
- Balloons (one per child)
- Papier mâché
- Paint and brushes
- Collage materials, e.g. sequins, felt shapes

Approach

1. Blow up a balloon and cover with several layers of papier mâché.
2. When dry, pop the balloon inside and decorate. Look at the elaborate patterns of Fabergé eggs for inspiration.
3. Provide collage materials for the children to decorate their eggs.

Cross-curricular Links

- **Food and Technology** – Study the special foods associated with Easter; for example, hot cross buns. Discuss how they are a Good Friday tradition and that they are divided into four to symbolise the cross at Calvary, the hill where Jesus was Crucified.
- **Design and Technology** – Look at the packaging of mass-produced Easter eggs. Discuss the amount of card and plastic used and whether it can be recycled etc. Discuss the environmental issues surrounding excess packaging. Challenge the children to design and make an Easter egg box that uses the minimum amount of materials.
- **Maths** – Weigh a chocolate Easter egg and compare its weight and value against a traditional chocolate bar.

World Book Day (Worldwide)

World Book Day was introduced by UNESCO (United Nations Education Scientific and Cultural Organisation) as a worldwide celebration of books and reading. It takes place in the UK and Ireland on the first Thursday in March but most other countries celebrate it on 23 April, St George's Day. The connection between 23 April and books has its origins in Catalonia in Spain. Here it is traditional for roses and books to be given as gifts to loved ones and so it became part of the St George's Day celebrations. When the World Book Day was first introduced, UNESCO decided it would be celebrated on this day not only because of the Catalonian festival but also because the date was the anniversary of the birth and death of William Shakespeare.

The main aim of the World Book Day is to encourage children to experience the joy of books and reading. School children are given a World Book Day book token that can be exchanged for one of the specially produced World Book Day books.

Alphabet Book

Resources

- Copy of *An Alphabet by Peter Blake* or images from the book (2008, Paul Stolper)
- Collection of 'found' imagery from magazines, comic, e.g. old cards, newspaper text or headlines, photographs
- Collage materials
- Paper, glue and scissors
- Paint

Approach

1. Peter Blake was born in 1932 and was a key figure of the Pop Art movement in the 1960s. He was best known for designing the album cover for the Beatles' *Sgt Pepper's Lonely Hearts Club Band* (1967). His work was usually in collage, adding popular artefacts such as magazine cuttings and 'found' imagery. Peter Blake's book *An Alphabet by Peter Blake* is a collection of colourful silkscreen prints, one for each letter of the alphabet, and was originally printed in 1991.
2. Look at pictures from *An Alphabet by Peter Blake* and talk about the Pop Art movement and Blake's work within it. Discuss the medium he uses and how his collages are put together using magazine cuttings and other images.
3. Provide the children with a collection of collage materials, paper, paint, scissors etc. Give each child a letter and ask them to sketch out possible designs with suitable images.
4. Allow the use of a computer to print out different fonts of the same letter to add to the collage.
5. Collect all the letters together and reproduce an alphabet book.

Book Characters

Resources

- Illustrations of children's book characters
- Paint and brushes
- Cartridge paper

Approach

1 Encourage the children to bring to school some pictures of their favourite book characters. Discuss what they like about the character and all the different styles of illustrations.
2 Provide paint and cartridge paper for the children to copy their character.
3 Display the characters with book reviews celebrating World Book Day.
4 Alternatively, the children could create their own book characters for a display.

Cross-curricular Links

- **Literacy**
  - – Write a letter to a book character.
  - – Write book reviews to share with the class.
  - – Read biographies of writers and illustrators.
  - – Design own book characters and write stories.
  - – Invite an author into school and interview him or her.
- **Design and Technology** – Study different formats of books and make your own book, such as pop-up books for young children. Write stories about different characters to put in the books.

May Day (Worldwide)

The first of May is May Day and is a festival that marks the arrival of warmer weather, new life and growth. In the past, the Celtic people split the year into just two seasons – summer and winter. The Celts celebrated the first day of May with the Beltane festival, named after Beli or Belinus, a Celtic sun god whose name meant 'bright fire'. A lot of customs from this time continue today. One of these is the making of a maypole from a tree trunk decorated with long, colourful ribbons. Each dancer holds a ribbon and dances around the pole. Some people celebrate May Day with a figure of a Green Man covered in leaves to represent the growth of plants and trees. May Day dances are performed by morris dancers, who are traditionally men. The stomping of feet and banging of sticks by the dancers was supposed to frighten away the evil spirits of winter and bring a good summer.

The nearest Monday to 1 May is now a holiday in the UK. In 1889 an organisation of workers decided there should be a holiday, an international workers' holiday to be known as 'labour day'. This day is celebrated in many cities around the world with parades in countries such as China and Russia, where it has become an important national holiday.

St Basil's Cathedral

Resources

- Pictures of St Basil's cathedral
- Paint and brushes
- Cartridge paper
- Collage materials, e.g. felt, sequins

Approach

1 In many countries, May Day is a secular national holiday and is celebrated as international Labour Day. It is a totally unrelated to May Day as a festival marking the arrival of spring. Talk to the children about these two different aspects of May Day, its histories and present customs.

2 Show the children pictures of Moscow and St Basil's cathedral in Red Square. Explain that on May Day large military parades are held in this capital city to celebrate Labour Day.

3 Discuss the extravagant and brightly coloured swirling domes. Ask the children to choose a part of the building they particularly like and, working as a group, create a display showing 'St Basil's cathedral' using a variety of media.

Green Man

Resources

- Plastic masks
- Sheet of card
- Fabric or real leaves
- Paint and glue

Approach

1. Explain to the children that there are many customs associated with May Day, one of which is the dressing of a figure of a green man in leaves to represent the growth of new plants and trees.
2. Give the children a sheet of card (one per group) and a plastic mask. Ask the children to attach the leaves using strips of glued paper, then paint and decorate the man's face.

Cross-curricular Links

- **PE** – Many May Day traditions involve dancing. Investigate maypole dancing and morris dancing. Formal country dances can be learned and performed to the school.
- **Geography** – In the past it was considered lucky for young girls to wash their faces in the morning dew on 1 May. It was said that anyone who did so would have a beautiful complexion throughout the year. Research typical weather sayings associated with May, such as 'A swarm of bees in May is worth a load of hay'. Discuss the origins and possible meanings of weather lore.

Bun Bang Fai (Thailand)

Bun Bang Fai takes place in north-eastern Thailand every year in the second week of May. This rocket festival and has been celebrated for centuries. According to legend there was once a rain god named Vassakan who loved to be worshipped with fire. The local people created a rocket or 'Bang Fai' to send up into the sky where the god resided. In Thailand, the month of May is the beginning of the rainy season and the people hope that Vassakan, the rain god, will bless them with plenty of rain for their crops. The festival lasts two days and villagers dress in colourful traditional costumes. On the second day of the festival the rockets, some as long as 9 metres, are taken to the launch site. Buddhist monks bless the rockets and the rocket that reaches the greatest height is declared the winner. The rockets are all home-made out of natural materials, such as bamboo, and are brightly coloured.

Rockets

Resources

- Pictures of decorated rockets at the festival
- Cardboard tubes or pieces of bamboo
- Sketching paper and pencils
- Paint and brushes
- Glue and scissors
- Collage materials

Approach

1 Show the children a map of the world and point out the location of Thailand. Discuss its climate and agriculture. Discuss the festival of Bun Bang Fai and its origins.
2 Give each child a cardboard tube or, if possible, a small piece of bamboo.
3 Look at pictures of decorated rockets at the festival and ask the children to sketch some ideas on a piece of paper.
4 Provide a variety of collage materials and paint to decorate the rockets (if using bamboo pieces mix some PVA glue with the paint to help it set on the smooth surface).
5 As a group activity make a large rocket using larger cardboard or bamboo tubes.

Bun Bang Fai Rocket

Resources

- Pictures of decorated rockets at the festival
- Paper
- Sheet of cardboard
- Balsa wood
- Wood strips
- Coloured matchsticks
- Glue

Approach

1 Show the children pictures of rockets made for the Bun Bang Fai festival. Look at the designs, patterns and colours and explain that on the festival day the rockets are paraded to the launch site with people dressed in colourful costumes with music and dancing accompanying the procession.

2 Give the children a piece of paper to design a rocket out of wood strips and coloured matchsticks.

3 Transfer the design to a rocket shape cut out of a sheet of cardboard or balsa wood.

Cross-curricular Links

- **Geography** – Research the weather conditions of Thailand, especially the rainfall. Make charts to show seasonal weather patterns.
- **Music** – Chanting or singing for the rocket festival is traditional. One person is the lead singer who chants and others follow. The themes of the songs are usually about the villagers' daily lives. Research some songs associated with the festival. Children could write their own and perform them.

Wesak (Buddhism)

Wesak is a Buddhist festival celebrated on the day of the full moon in the month of Visakha or Vaishaka in May. At this time Theravada Buddhists celebrate the birth, enlightenment and death of Gautama Buddha. The festival lasts for three days and temples and homes are decorated with flowers, lanterns and lights. As a symbol of the Buddha's concern, love and compassion for human kind and living things, captured birds and fish are released and gifts are given to the poor.

Fish Bowl

Resources

- Sheet of acetate
- Glass paints and outliners
- Pictures of tropical fish
- Paper and felt pens

Approach

1. Talk to the children about the festival of Wesak. Discuss why captured birds and fish are set free during the festival. Remind the children of the Buddhist teachings of respect for others and kindness to all living things and explore ways that these ideals can be applied to animals.
2. Show the children pictures of tropical fish that are often put into aquariums.
3. Give the children a large sheet of paper and ask them to draw pictures of fish having researched different shapes and colours first.
4. Cover the paper with a sheet of acetate and trace over the outline of each fish with a glass outliner.
5. Allow the outliner to dry and then paint the fish with glass paints.
6. Display the acetate fish over a blue piece of paper cut into the shape of a fish bowl.

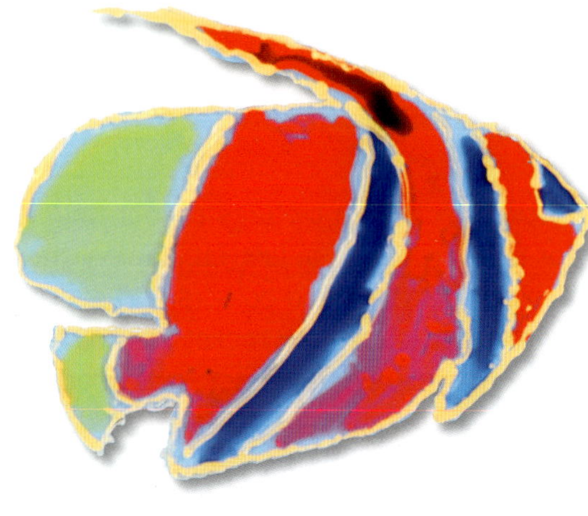

Lotus Flower

Resources

- Paper or card
- Glue
- Pictures of lotus flowers
- Silk and silk paints

Approach

1 Explain to the children that during the festival of Wesak, lotus buds are offered at temples to celebrate the birth and enlightenment of Gautama Buddha. The lotus is important because it is the symbol of growing and reaching enlightenment; the lotus flower starts as a small flower at the bottom of a pond and slowly grows through the water continually moving towards the light. Once it reaches the surface it blossoms into a beautiful flower.

2 Show the children pictures of lotus flowers and explain that it is rather like a water lily.

3 Demonstrate how to fold paper to make a lotus flower. Using a square piece of paper, fold it diagonally, first across one diagonal and then across the other. Unfold. Fold the corners into the middle and turn the paper over. Fold corners into the middle again. Slide a finger into each flap on the lower side of the paper and push upwards so that the points of the corners meet in the middle. Pull out the flaps and cut along the diagonal crease to form a spread of petals.

4 Encourage children to experiment with their own designs for a 3D lotus flower.

5 Use silk and silk paints to create delicate fabric designs of lotus flowers.

6 Display the silk paintings with the 3D paper flowers.

Cross-curricular Links

- **Science/Literacy** – Look at the natural habitats of various caged animals in zoos. Prepare an argument 'for' or 'against' keeping animals in zoos and debate the issues as a class.

Well Dressing (Christianity)

Between the months of May and September, some villages in Derbyshire, England, 'dress' their village wells with pictures made from local plant life. The origins of this festival are a mystery but it is thought to date back to pagan times when rituals were performed to give thanks for fresh water. Water was such a vital commodity that giving thanks for a clean supply has always been a strong custom. Well dressing today usually has a strong religious theme, often depicting scenes from the Bible. The flower petals for the dressing are set in clay-filled wooden trays and can take a team of people up to seven days to complete. When the clay has set, the dressing is displayed near an ancient source of water and is usually blessed on the same day. The dressings only last for about a week before the clay dries and cracks and the flowers fade.

Circular Collage

Resources

- Pictures of well dressings
- Collection of peas, beans, lentils and other collage materials
- Sheet of circular card
- Glue and glue spreaders

Approach

1. Show the children pictures of well dressings and discuss the history of the festival and the designs.
2. On a circular piece of card, encourage the children to draw a design for a well dressing collage.
3. Working from the centre of the card outwards, stick collage leaves and flowers onto the card, overlapping the petals to allow full coverage.

Well Dressing Display

Resources

- Pictures of well dressings
- Texts from the Bible or secular celebratory texts
- Collection of peas, beans, lentils and other collage materials
- Sketch paper
- Large sheet of card
- Glue and glue spreaders

Approach

1. Look at pictures of well dressings. Choose a theme for the display – if choosing a religious theme, provide copies of Bible stories (or other religious texts) to read.
2. On paper, encourage the children to work out a design for the display.
3. Sketch out the design onto a large sheet of card.
4. Working from the base of the card upwards, stick collage leaves and flowers onto the card, overlapping the petals to allow full coverage.

Cross-curricular Links

- **History** – Study the story of the Plague of Eyam. Eyam is a village in Derbyshire famous for its well-dressing festival. It is equally famous for being the 'plague village' that went into quarantine in 1665 when the plague was transported to the people of Eyam in a parcel of cloth.
- **Geography** – Study how we get our fresh water supply. Investigate diseases associated with dirty, infected water.

Tanabata (Japan)

Tanabata is the Japanese Star Festival and is celebrated on 7 July. It recalls the story of an oxherder and a weaving maiden living in space. They were so much in love that they couldn't do their jobs properly, so the gods separated them and put them on opposite sides of the Amanogawa River or Milky Way. Once a year on the seventh day of the seventh month they are allowed to meet. In Japan, people celebrate this day by writing wishes, sometimes in the form of poetry on small strips of paper. These wishes are tied to bamboo sticks and waved at stars during this festival in the hope that the wish will come true. Fireworks are lit and many outdoor stalls sell festival food.

Paper Weaving

Resources

- Sheets of cartridge paper
- Strips of coloured paper
- Paint and brushes

Approach

1. Tell the story of the oxherder and the weaving maiden and talk about the festival of Tanabata.
2. Give the children a sheet of cartridge paper each and ask them to paint all the paper in a bright and colourful pattern.
3. Vertically cut strips in the cartridge paper.
4. Weave the coloured strips of paper into the cartridge paper.
5. Display the weaving pictures on a brightly coloured paper 'woven' background.

Wool Weaving on Grids

Resources

- Plastic weaving grids
- Wool
- Wide-eyed needles
- Pen
- Sellotape®

Approach

1 With a pen, sketch a pattern of a star onto the plastic grid.
2 Demonstrate how to weave the wool in and out of the grid to fill in the pattern.
3 Change the wool colour as required and stick down loose ends with Sellotape® on reverse.

Wool Weaving on Looms

Resources

- Weaving loom
- Wool
- Large bodkin needles

Approach

1 Introduce the terms 'warp threads' and 'weft threads'. Warp threads are the vertical threads and weft threads are horizontal threads woven across the warp.
2 Weave blue threads in and out across the weaving loom tying on extra threads when needed.
3 When the weaving has been completed, cut the warp threads at the back of the loom.
4 Display the weaving behind a cut-out cardboard star.

Cross-curricular Links

- **Literacy** – Write 'wish messages' on strips of paper. Talk about the different types of wishes; for example, for themselves, their family, for the world.

St Swithun's Day (England)

St Swithun's Day is on 15 July. It is well known for the British weather proverb that states that if it rains on St Swithun's Day, it will rain for the following 40 days and 40 nights:

St Swithun's Day if thou dost rain
For forty days it will remain
St Swithun's Day if thou be fair
For forty days 'twill rain na mair'

St Swithun was an Anglo-Saxon Bishop of Winchester who was born around the year 800 and died on 2 July 862. Legend says that on his deathbed he asked to be buried outdoors in the churchyard where 'sweet rain from heaven' could fall on his grave. For nine years his wishes were granted and then the monks, feeling it wasn't a fitting resting place for St Swithun, decided to move his grave to a splendid ornate shrine within Winchester Cathedral. According to the myth, the move was delayed by torrential, incessant rain, which continued for 40 days – a sign of St Swithun's displeasure at the move. The monks eventually decided against removing his remains.

Renoir Umbrellas

Resources

- Copy of Pierre- Auguste Renoir's painting *The Umbrellas* (about 1881–86)
- Cartridge paper
- Paints and brushes
- Withy canes
- Tissue paper
- PVA glue

Approach

1 Weather is a popular topic in primary schools and there are many examples of artwork inspired by rain, storm and puddles. Introduce the children to the artist Pierre-Auguste Renoir (1841–1919). He was part of the Impressionist movement and painted the picture *The Umbrellas* about 1881. Talk to the children about the painting and identify all the different shades of blue within it.

2 Ask the children to highlight areas of interest and recreate it on cartridge paper. Demonstrate how to create different shades of blue by putting the white paint in the palette first and adding various amounts of blue and other colours to it.

3 Display with 3D umbrellas made from withy cane frames with tissue paper covers.

Escher Puddles

Resources

- Picture of M.C. Escher's *Puddle* (1952)
- Cartridge paper
- Black ink, pens and brushes

Approach

1 Show the children a copy of *Puddle* by M.C. Escher (1898–1972) and point out how the image of the trees has been reflected in the puddle. Discuss the background and reflection in the puddles.

2 If possible, take the children outside to observe the reflections of trees in puddles. Make sketches.

4 Give the children a piece of cartridge paper and ask them to create a background around a puddle.

5 Referring to their sketches of reflection of trees in puddles, use ink to create an Escher-style puddle. Encourage the children to put in details of branches using the ink pens.

Cross-curricular Links

- **Geography/Literacy** – Read some weather proverbs and investigate if there is any truth in them. For example:

  Red sky at night, shepherds delight.
  Red sky in the morning, Shepherd's warning.

  Oak before ash, in for a splash.
  Ash before oak, in for a soak.

  Rain before seven, fine before eleven.

- **Science** – Research some traditional methods of measuring temperature and humidity; for example, it is said that if a pine cone is put outside, it will change when humidity increases as it closes up in moist weather to protect the seeds.

Eisteddfod (Wales)

An Eisteddfod is a festival of music, song and poetry. It is an arts festival held in the first week of August when Welsh people compete in contests to find the best writers, composers and performers. It is a celebration of Welsh customs and heritage and people wear their traditional costumes and speak in the Welsh language. All the competitions are in Welsh.

There is also an Eisteddfod held twice a year in Patagonia in South America. It started in the 1880s and includes competitions in music, poetry and recitation in Welsh, Spanish and English. The winner of the best poem in Spanish receives a silver crown.

Silver Crown

Resources

- Silver card
- Purple fabric
- Sequins
- Glue and scissors

Approach

1 Explain that during an Eisteddfod people take part in competitions to find the best writers, poets and musicians. The winner is awarded a silver crown.
2 Make a crown using silver card and purple fabric. Decorate with sequins.
3 As a class or school, hold an Eisteddfod-style festival and write poems, sing songs etc.
4 Award the silver crown to the winner of an Eisteddfod writing competition.

Celtic Patterns

The Iron Age Celts were a tribe of people who lived across Europe about two thousand years ago. They migrated and gradually moved to England and Wales about 500–100 BC. They were fierce warriors who lived in small farming communities and were famous for their beautiful ornamental art. Their culture lives on in language, music, song and literature. The annual Eisteddfod embraces all aspects of Welsh culture, much of which lies rooted in Celtic history.

Resources

- Examples of Celtic art
- Pieces of square cotton fabric
- Fabric dye
- Elastic bands
- Pieces of cartridge paper
- Card and scissors
- Paint and brushes

Approach

1 The origins of the Celts dates back to prehistoric times and there are many different styles associated with different tribes and settlements. However, geometric designs have always featured prominently in Celtic art with interwoven spirals, knot-work, crosses, scrolls and chevrons making ornamental patterns.

2 Give each child a square piece of fabric. Demonstrate how to tie the fabric using elastic bands.

3 Put the fabric in dye, rinse and leave to dry.

4 When dry, untie the squares of cloth and iron them.

5 Show the children examples of Celtic art and ask them to sketch a design on a piece of cartridge paper.

6 When the children are happy with their design, transfer it onto card. Cut out the design and stick it onto a piece of card. Allow to dry.

7 Paint the card and print the design onto the fabric.

Cross-curricular Links

- **History** – Study the legend of King Arthur. It is generally believed that not only was King Arthur an actual historical figure but he was also first mentioned in Welsh poetry.
  – St David is the patron saint of Wales. He died on 1 March AD 589. Research his life.
- **Design and Technology** – The leek has been an emblem of Wales since the middle of the sixteenth century. Plan and eat recipes using this vegetable.

Esala Perahera (Buddhism)

Esala Perahera is a Buddhist festival held every year in Sri Lanka in August. It is their main midsummer festival and lasts for ten nights. The highlight comes on the night of the full moon when there is a magnificent torchlight procession of over 100 elephants. At the centre of the procession is a grand elephant, the Maligawa Tusker. His tusks are covered in jewels and he is clothed in a richly decorated costume for the occasion. Buddhists honour holy relics and the Maligawa Tusker carries a replica of Buddha's sacred tooth in a golden cachet. Many different groups of dancers, acrobats, flame-throwers and drummers take part in the festival, which is thought to date back to the third century BC and honours the Buddha.

Silk Elephant Hanging

Resources

- Silk – one large and one smaller piece (per child)
- Silk paints
- Silk gutta
- Pictures of decorated elephants
- Brushes
- Card
- Sequins
- Sellotape®

Approach

1. Talk about the festival and research some traditional elephant costumes. Ask the children to sketch some ideas and discuss possible colours for a silk elephant hanging.
2. On a piece of card draw a picture of the Maligawa Tusker. Press hard with the pencil so that the design will show through the silk fabric.
3. Place the silk on top of the design and tape around the edges.
4. Trace around the lines of the drawing in silk gutta, making sure that the silk gutta completely encloses areas of the silk.
5. Give children a smaller individual piece of silk to design a decorative boarder in the same way.
6. Paint the designs with silk paints and leave to dry.
7. Gently peel off the silk from the cardboard and mount it on a new piece of card, embellish with sequins.

Esala Perahera Display

Resources

- Coloured wrapping paper
- String
- Small piece of cardboard
- Scissors and glue
- Paint and brushes
- Sticky paper and collage paper

Approach

1. Draw a design of an elephant on a small sheet of card.
2. Cover the design with string and allow to dry.
3. Paint over the string and press down firmly onto the coloured wrapping paper.
4. Decorate with shapes cut out of collage paper.
5. Display with brightly coloured balloons decorated with sticky paper.

Cross-curricular Links

- **Literacy** – Read stories featuring elephants such as Rudyard Kipling's *Just So* story 'How the elephant got its trunk'. Ask the children to write their own 'just so' stories. Read extracts from *The Story of Babar the little Elephant* by F. Poulenc or *Elmer the Elephant* by D. McKee (Red Fox).
- **PE/Music** – Listen to the elephant march from *The Carnival of the Animals* by Camille Saint-Saëns (1835–1921). Explore the movements of an elephant and in dance prepare an elephant march.

The Olympic Games (Worldwide)

The Olympic Games is the biggest sporting festival in the world and is held every four years in a different country. The first Olympics were held almost 3000 years ago in a place called Olympia on the south-western Greek mainland. The games were originally held in honour of the Greek god Zeus. The ancient Olympics consisted of just one event, a sprint race called the Stade, which was run over a distance of about 190 metres. The modern Olympics were first held in April 1896 in Athens, Greece. The man behind the event was a young French baron called Pierre de Coubertin (1863–1937). He believed that sport could inspire the best in people and bring nations together. Over 65 different sports are now played and over 200 nations take part. The Olympic symbol is five rings interconnected with three on the top and two on the bottom. At least one of the five colours of the rings – blue, black, red, yellow and green – appears in all the flags of the competing nations. The five rings represent the five continents involved in the Olympic Games – Asia, Europe, Oceania, Africa and the Americas. The Olympic motto is *Citius Altius Fortius*, which means 'swifter, higher, stronger'.

Olympic Rings

Resources

- Blue, black, red, yellow and green dye
- Circles of cotton fabric
- Elastic bands and dried peas

Approach

1 Place a dried pea in the centre of the circle, gather the fabric around it and tie the elastic band. Leave a small space and tie another band. Repeat until the edge of the circle is reached.
2 Place the fabric in the bucket of dye and leave for at least an hour.
3 When dry, iron flat (only an adult should use the iron).
4 Use as part of the Painted Design display (page 53).

Painted Design

Resources

- Circular cartridge paper
- Blue, black, red, yellow and green paint
- Brushes
- Circular templates

Approach

1 The Olympic flag with its interconnected rings was designed by Pierre de Coubertin. Discuss with the children how the colours are representative of the colours of the different national flags and the symbolism of the linked circles.
2 Provide the children with different templates of circles. Ask the children to create a circular pattern of interconnecting overlapping rings.
3 Paint in the Olympic ring colours.
4 Display with the tie and dye circles (page 52).

Commemorative Stamps

Resources

- Cartridge paper
  Greek vase template
- Examples of ancient Greek vases and pottery
- Examples of postage stamps
- Paint and brushes

Approach

1 Talk to the children about how the ancient Olympics took place in the city of Olympia in 776 BC. Discuss how a lot of our knowledge about the ancient Olympic games is based on evidence from vases and pottery. Show pictures of ancient Greek vases and describe the scenes portrayed. Discuss the movement and posture of the athletes.
2 Explain that the children are going to design a commemorative stamp using some images from archaeological evidence of the first Olympic games.
3 Provide the children with a template of a Greek vase. Refer to the pictures of Olympic athletes on the Greek vases and draw a design in pencil. Paint in black poster paint.
4 Discuss what images could be used to represent the modern Olympic Games on commemorative stamps.

Cross-curricular Links

- **Literacy**
  - *Citius, Altius Fortius* is the motto of the Olympic games. It means 'swifter, higher, stronger'. Create haiku poetry based on the meaning of the motto.
  - Write a speech for the opening ceremony to be read by the president of the IOC (International Olympic Committee).
  - Make posters to advertise the games.
- **Maths** – Study Olympic records in various events. Compare records of the past and present.

Raksha Bandhan (Hinduism)

Raksha Bandhan is a Hindu festival, which many Sikhs also celebrate. Raksha Bandhan means 'bond of protection' and is celebrated on the day of the full moon of Shravana, which can fall in July or August. The festival celebrates the love between brothers and sisters and involves sisters giving a bracelet to their brothers. The bracelet signifies the sister's love and devotion to her brother. The festival custom is said to relate to an ancient Hindu story when Indra was given a threaded bracelet by his wife Indrani to protect him in his battle against the demons. According to legend, this protective thread strengthened Indra and the gods vanquished the demons and Indra regained his kingdom.

Before the giving of bracelets, a sister places a tilak (a sacred mark) of coloured powder or paste on her brother's forehead and in return a brother blesses his sister, promises to protect her and gives her a small gift.

Weaving Bracelets

Resources

- Threads in different colours
- Beads and sequins
- Pipe cleaners
- Scissors and glue

Approach

1. Talk to the children about the symbol of the Rakhi bracelet. Rakhi bracelets are usually made from silk thread and decorated with beads or motifs.
2. If possible, show examples of Rakhi bracelets or, alternatively, pictures of them.
3. Demonstrate how to plait threads by choosing three bunches of threads in different colours. Tie at one end leaving quite a lot of loose threads before the knot and at the end of the tying off the knot. Thread beads onto the ends and tie another knot to prevent them from falling off. For younger children, thread beads onto pipe cleaners to make bracelets.
4. Encourage the children to experiment with different ways to make Rakhi bracelets.

Toran Door Hanging

A Toran is an Indian door hanging for decorating the home during Hindu festivals. It is strung across the doorframe and gives a friendly, warm welcome to guests who visit during festival times. Many different patterns and themes are used, colours are chosen with care and the design is embellished with mirrors, sequins and beads.

Resources

- Examples of decorated Torans
- Felt and collage material
- Sequins, beads and mirrors
- Glue and scissors
- Paper and pencils

Approach

1 Research some Toran designs and discuss their significance to the Hindu religion. Look at various symbols on Torans; for example, the elephant signifies strength and is an important symbol as it is the vehicle of Lord Indra, king of gods.

2 Give the children a piece of paper and as a group project, experiment with some Toran designs.

3 Transfer designs to a Toran cut-out of coloured felt.

Cross-curricular Links

- **Food Technology** – Sweets and chocolate have always been part of the traditional celebrations of Raskha Bandhan. Dried fruits are also given as gifts. Design and make up boxes of dried fruits, write messages in the boxes for sisters to give to brothers and brothers to give to sisters. Discuss alternative recipients for children without siblings.
- **PSHCE** – Although Raksha Bandhan is a festival celebrating the bond between brothers and sisters, it is also essentially bringing families together and wishing each other happiness and protection. This feeling of goodwill often extends to close friends and neighbours.

La Tomatina (Spain)

La Tomatina or the tomato throwing festival takes place in the Spanish town of Buñol every year on the last Wednesday in August. Its origins are neither religious nor political and is thought to date back to sometime during the 1940s. There are several different stories of how it started, one being that during an annual parade of carnival figures passing through the streets of Buñol, a mass brawl broke out during which the offenders used tomatoes from a nearby stall as ammunition. The following year on the same last Wednesday of August, the people involved in the fight returned to relive the incident as they had had so much fun! The police intervened and for a while La Tomatina was outlawed, as the authorities feared it was getting out of control. However, they had little success and eventually in 1959 the event was given an official status but the authorities insisted on certain restrictions on activities. These rules included:

- Only throwing ripe tomatoes and not rock-hard green tomatoes.
- Always crush the tomatoes in your hand before throwing them.
- Throwing must start and finish at the sound of the rocket.
- Nobody should try to rip anyone's T-shirt!

3D Tomatoes

Resources

- Balloons
- Papier mâché
- Card
- Paint and brushes
- Collage material
- Mod roc or sticky paper

Approach

1. Blow up balloons, cover with papier mâché and allow to dry.
2. Cut in half and attach to a large sheet of card with strips of mod roc or sticky paper.
3. Make stalks and leaves out of mod roc.
4. Paint and display with recipe cards of tomato dishes and information about La Tomatina.

Tomato Collage

Resources

- Tomatoes
- Drawing pencils
- Mixed media – paints, crayons, fabric, paper
- Cartridge paper
- Large sheet of card
- Glue

Approach

1 Display the tomatoes so that each child can carefully study their shape and colour.
2 Discuss the composition of still-life art, explore the textural qualities, how the light falls on the tomatoes etc. Encourage the children to record carefully what they see.
3 Develop their observational drawings into a mixed media collage. Display as a group collage.

Cross-curricular Links

- **Science** – Study the growing conditions for tomatoes; for example, ideal temperature. Discuss why they are mainly imported into this country. Photograph the tomato collage and make into seed packets with appropriate growing instructions.
- **Art/ICT** – Look at the pop art work of American artist Andy Warhol (1928–1987). Design a poster similar to his works, such as *Soup Cans 100 Campbells* (1962) or *Campbells Soup (Tomato)* (1968).

Trung Thu (Vietnam)

Trung Thu is an ancient Vietnamese festival traditionally held on the fifteenth day of the eighth lunar month (September). This mid-autumn festival revolves around children and it is said that the festival originally came about as a way for parents to make up for lost time with their children after the harvest season. It is held under the full moon, which is brighter than at any other time of the year and represents fullness and prosperity of life. Children parade on the streets carrying lanterns of many shapes, including star-shaped lanterns that spin when a candle is inserted.

Trung Thu festivities often include unicorn dancers who dance to the sound of drums and cymbals. Moon cakes are a traditional part of the festival and contain unusual sweet fillings such as sugar with meat.

Star Lantern

Resources

- Pictures of lanterns
- Bamboo hoop
- Bamboo canes
- Masking tape
- Cellophane or coloured plastic
- Crêpe paper

Approach

1 The Trung Thu festivals celebrate the beauty of the full moon and children carry lanterns in a night-time parade. Candles are put inside the lantern, which are made from a bamboo frame with plastic stretched across in the shape of a star. Talk to the children about the Trung Thu festival and look at examples of lanterns.
2 Cover a bamboo hoop with crêpe paper.
3 Make a star out of canes and attach to the hoop using masking tape.
4 Cover the star with coloured cellophane or plastic and decorate.

Star Patterns

Resources

- Art straws
- Masking tape
- Tissue paper
- Sequins and collage materials
- Scissors and glue

Approach

1 Demonstrate how to make a star shape using art straws. Join the art straws together with masking tape.
2 Cover the stars with tissue paper and decorate.
3 Use the decorated stars to make smaller lanterns on display with poems or writing about the Trung Thu festival.

Cross-curricular Links

- **Design and Technology/ICT** – Moon cakes are a traditional part of the Trung Thu festival. They sometimes contain unusual sweet fillings. Research recipes for moon cakes on the Internet. Try to make a variety and discuss which are the favourite fillings in the class.

European Day of Languages (Europe)

The European Day of Languages is held annually on 26 September. It is a Council of Europe initiative and aims to increase awareness and appreciation of all languages. There are over 200 European languages and the day aims to encourage the importance of language learning and to promote better understanding of cultural differences. It is celebrated in over 40 countries across Europe. Various events are organised, such as radio and television programmes, language classes and conferences. There is a European Day of Languages logo and many online resources.

European Union Design

The European Union flag is a symbol of Europe's unity. It is a circle of 12 yellow stars on an azure blue sky. It was created in 1955 by the Council of Europe and adopted by the European Union in the 1980s. The number of stars does not represent the number of nations but symbolises the idea of unity, harmony and perfection.

Resources

- Picture of European Union flag
- Star templates
- Yellow and blue paint and brushes
- Yellow and blue paper
- Scissors and glue

Approach

1 Show the children a picture of the European Union flag and discuss its meaning.
2 Provide star templates and ask the children to design an alternative new flag for the European Union.
3 Cut out coloured paper to make the stars or paint them.

European Flags

Resources

- Examples of European flags
- Paper
- Wax pastels
- Hand template

Approach

1 Explain that a flag is usually an abstract combination of different colours. Provide examples of different European flags, discuss the colours and explore any particular characteristics of the countries they represent.
2 Give the children a piece of paper and draw round a hand template.
3 Ask the children to mix and match designs and colours of flags and create a picture putting one design inside the hand shape and another as a background, symbolising unity of nations.

Cross-curricular Links

- **Geography** – Map all the countries in Europe and list all the different languages that are spoken in these countries.
- **Design and Technology** – Have food tasting sessions from different countries.
- **Music** – Listen to different types of music associated with different European countries.
- **PE** – Try traditional dancing from different countries, such as Flamenco (Spain).

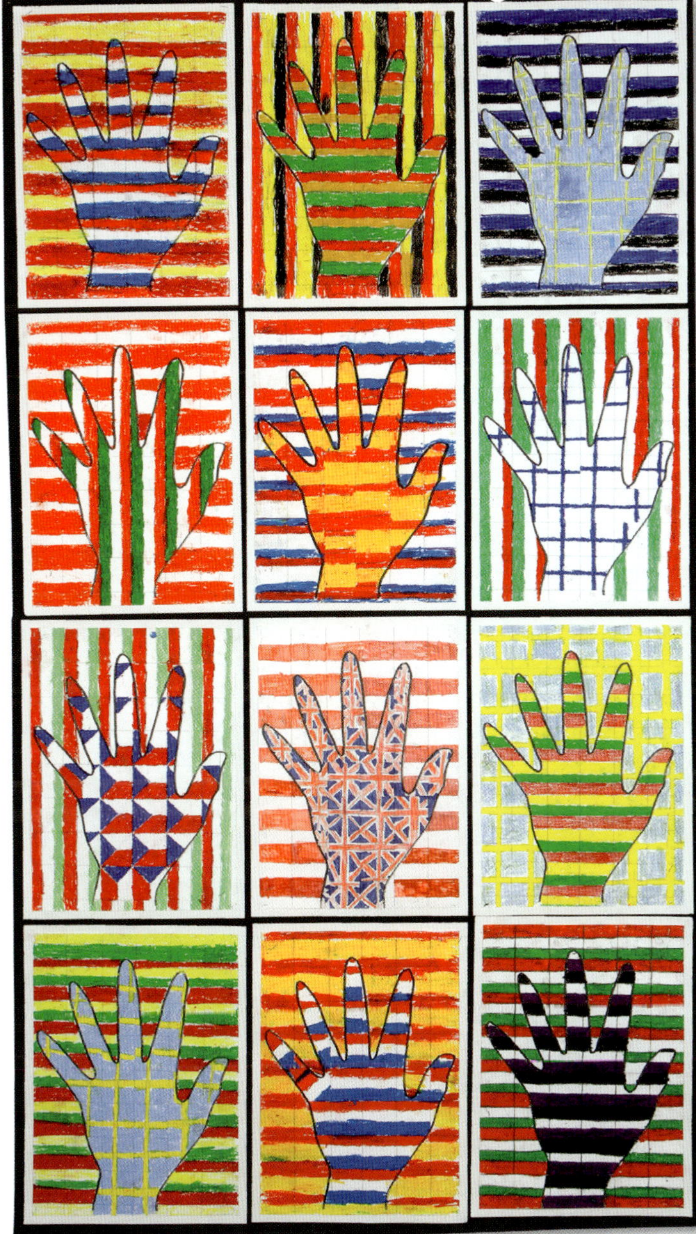

Harvest Festival (Christianity)

Harvest festival is celebrated in the Christian church in autumn and dates back to a time when success of a good harvest governed the lives of people and their animals for the following year. Harvest festivals are traditionally held on or near the full moon that occurs closest to the autumn equinox, in September or October. People bring gifts to church for the harvest festival. In the past these gifts were flowers, fruit or vegetables but very often today they include non-perishable items, which are easier to distribute to those in need.

The London tradition of the Pearly Kings and Queens (Pearlies) was started in 1875 by a small boy called Henry Croft. Henry was born in 1862 and was raised in an orphanage, which he left at the age of 13 to become a road sweeper. He also worked as a rat catcher in the market of Somers Town. Costermongers (street traders) on the market decorated their trousers and waistcoats with a row of pearl buttons down the seams. Henry was fascinated not only by their outfits but also how they looked out for each other if any of them were in difficulty. Henry decided he would like to help the children back at the orphanage, so he totally covered a suit in pearly buttons and became an instant attraction. He raised a lot of money for charity during his lifetime and Pearlies hold a harvest festival on the first Sunday in October. The service is held at St Martin on the Field's Church in London and the Pearlies attend the service dressed in their outfits, which can have as many as 30,000 buttons on them and weigh as much as 30 kilograms or more.

Pearly Hat

Resources

- Felt black hat
- Pearl buttons
- Glue

Approach

1. Research information on the Internet about the London tradition of the Pearly Kings and Queens. Look at pictures and discuss their elaborate costumes.
2. Talk about their involvement with various charities and the harvest festival held on the first Sunday of October.
3. Provide felt hats (or alternatively 2D hats made from black card) and cover in pearl-coloured buttons.

Apple Pictures

Resources

- Photographs of apples
- Cartridge paper
- Paint and brushes

Approach

1 Discuss how and why Christians celebrate harvest. Explain that Christians like to say thank you to God for a good harvest. Explain how food and farming have changed over the years and we are no longer so reliant on a good harvest for our food because many foods are imported. However, the custom of thanksgiving for the good future of food continues today and is a chance to share prayers for others who are not so fortunate.

2 Give each child a piece of cartridge paper and a photograph of some apples to look at and discuss texture, colours etc.

3 Stick the photo onto the middle of the paper. Provide paint for the children to mix colours and extend the picture to the edge of the paper.

4 Draw and paint large apples to display with the photograph pictures.

Cross-curricular Links

- **Music**
  - Listen to the song 'John Barleycorn' (English folk song). Discuss the words and story. Make a new verse for the song.
  - Listen to the words and music of the hymn sung by Christians at harvest time, 'We Plough the Fields and Scatter'. Discuss its meaning and why it is sung at this festival.
- **Art** – In the past, the end of the harvest was celebrated with a meal called a harvest supper, which was eaten on Michaelmas Day. Michaelmas Day occurs on 29 September in the Christian calendar. It derives its name from the feast of St Michael and all angels. Michaelmas daisies were named as such because they usually flower around this time. Draw pictures of Michaelmas daisies.
- **History** – Research the story of the Pilgrim Fathers who sailed from England to America in the *Mayflower*. When the Pilgrim Fathers arrived in America, it was too late to sow crops that year and the Native Americans provided them with food, which helped them survive. The following year a successful harvest was gathered and the governor announced there would be a three-day festival of thanksgiving.

Chinese Moon Festival (Worldwide)

The Moon Festival, or Mid-Autumn Festival, is held on the fifteenth day of the eighth month of the Chinese year (September) and is to give thanks for a successful harvest. Traditionally, Chinese families will enjoy a special feast and decorate their houses with festive lanterns often shaped like an animal, bird or fish. The moon festival is mainly regarded as a festival for women as the Chinese call the moon the 'Queen of Heaven' and it symbolises beauty and elegance. On the night of the festival, the moon is at its brightest and roundest. People exchange sweet moon cakes and festival fruits, especially ones that are round like the moon, such as apples, peaches and pomegranates. There are many folk tales about Chang'e the lady on the moon and legend says that on this night children who make wishes to her will find their dreams come true.

Chinese Paper Cuts

Resources

- Paint and brushes
- Pictures of Chinese paper cuts
- Cartridge paper
- Scissors

Approach

1 Explain that the Chinese invented paper and during Chinese festivals paper cuts are used for decorating houses to bring good luck.

2 Arrange for the children to have a collection of paper cuts to study or pictures of paper cuts. Explain the history of the craft and how some designs have symbolic meaning, such as lions and tigers are symbols of courage and strength.

3 Allow the children to experiment with their own designs to celebrate the moon festival.

4 Paint and cut out parts of the design to look like paper cuts to create a display.

Marbling Moon Tangrams

Resources

- Marbling inks
- Water tray
- Cartridge paper
- Tangram sheet
- Examples of trangram puzzles
- Black paper
- Scissors

Approach

1 Demonstrate the process of creating marbling backgrounds by dropping marbling ink into water. Try combing into circular movements and the placing a piece of cartridge paper onto the ink to soak up the pattern.
2 When dry, cut the marbled paper into a circle to represent the full moon.
3 The tangram puzzle was invented in China 4000 years ago. The puzzle requires seven pieces to be used with no piece overlapping to create an arrangement. Give the children a copy of a tangram sheet (see example right) and examples of what can be made from the puzzle. Examples can be found on the Internet. Encourage the children to experiment with their own design using cut black paper shapes. When the children are happy with their design, stick it onto the marbling moon.

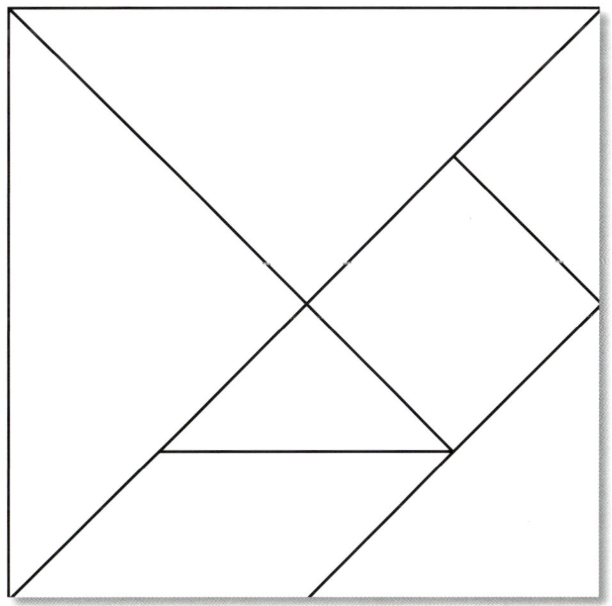

Cross-curricular Links

- **Literacy**
  - Read *The Moon Lady* by Amy Tan (Puffin). Ask the children to write their own version of the story.
  - The moon is a favourite subject for poets in China, read poems about the moon such as 'Silver' by Walter de la Mare (a version can be found on the Internet) and ask the children to compose their own.
  - Make paper cuts into cards to send on the moon festival.
  - Calligraphy is the art and skill of writing Chinese characters. Practise writing Chinese calligraphy, such as the word *moon*.

Eid ul-Fitr (Islam)

Ramadan is the ninth month in the Islamic calendar that comes before the festival of Eid ul-Fitr. Ramadan is a time of fasting and during this month Muslims do not eat food during daylight hours. Ramadan does not start on the same date each year because Muslims follow the lunar calendar. It usually falls between August and October. The festival of Eid starts with the first appearance of the new moon and is a festival of fast breaking. It is a family celebration where people go to the mosque and say special prayers. New clothes are worn, gifts are exchanged and money is given to charity. Children exchange gifts of sugar almonds in decorated boxes. The festival lasts for three days.

Decorated Boxes

Resources

- Ready-made boxes (or card and nets)
- Coloured paint and brushes

Approach

1. Talk to the children about the celebration of Eid and how people prepare special meals and take gifts of sweets and sugared almonds in decorated boxes to their friends.
2. If using a net, make up the boxes and leave to dry. Paint the background of the boxes.
3. When dry, decorate the boxes in Islamic-style patterns.

Islamic Patterns

Resources

- Examples of Islamic patterns
- Squared paper
- Cartridge paper
- Paint and brushes

Approach

1 Explain to the children that Muslims are people who follow the religion of Islam. Talk about the teachings of the Prophet Muhammad who lived between 570 and 632 CE.
2 People often exchange Eid cards and the greeting 'Eid Mubarak' (happy Eid) is exchanged. Show examples to the children.
3 Explain that Islamic designs are often geometric, made up of symmetrical colourful patterns. They do not include pictures of people or animals. Show examples.
4 Give the children squared cartridge paper to plan out their design.
5 Paint and either display as a celebration of Islamic design or transfer designs onto an Eid card.

Cross-curricular Links

- **Maths**
  - Experiment with different ways of making geometric symmetrical patterns.
  - Ramadan is the ninth month of the Islamic calendar. Study the lunar calendar and the fact that it is 11 days shorter than the Gregorian calendar, which has 365 (366 in a leap year). Discuss the differences.
- **RE** – Explore the reasons for fasting. Look at different religions and times of fasting. Make lists of positive reasons associated with fasting; for example, it helps to learn self-restraint and it helps to remember people who are hungry.

Diwali (Hinduism)

Diwali is the Hindu festival of light held at the start of the Hindu New Year in October or November. It celebrates the return of Rama and Sita to their kingdom after fourteen years in exile. The word 'Diwali' comes from 'Deepavali', which means a 'row of lights' and the candles of Diwali represents those that were lit to guide Rama and Sita back home. The festival is also in honour of the goddess Lakshmi, the wife of Vishnu, and people light divas (small clay lamps) in the hope that she will visit their homes and bring prosperity. Diwali lasts for five days. Homes are cleaned and decorated and lights are placed in windows. Presents and cards are given, special food is prepared and fireworks are lit.

Symbolically, Diwali represents the triumph of light over darkness, good over evil and it is a time to resolve differences and celebrate the bonds of friendship and family.

Rangoli Wall Hanging

Resources

- Examples of Rangoli patterns
- Squared paper
- Small square of cloth (one per child)
- Fabric paint and brushes

Approach

1. Rangoli are geometric designs made on the floors of houses to welcome the goddess Lakshmi at Diwali. Traditionally the patterns are drawn on the floor with chalk and coloured powders and have two axes of symmetry. Show the children examples of Rangoli patterns
2. On squared paper, demonstrate how to design a Rangoli pattern with two axes of symmetry.
3. Transfer the pattern onto a piece of cloth and paint.
4. Join all the pieces of cloth together to make a wall hanging.

Mehndi Collage

Resources

- Small squares of fabric
- Pictures of Mehndi patterns
- Paint and brushes
- Sequins

Approach

1 Mehndi patterns are a traditional decoration on hands and feet during Diwali. They are elaborate designs painted into the skin with henna dye. Look at examples of Mehndi patterns.
2 Give each child a small square of fabric and ask them to draw around one of their hands.
3 Decorate with a pattern of their choice and display all the squares together as a group collage.

Cross-curricular Links

- **Literacy**
  - Retell the story of Rama and Sita.
  - Make Diwali cards.
  - Act out the story of Rama and Sita returning to their kingdom after 14 years in exile.
- **Design and Technology** – Make traditional Indian sweets (mithai). As with all food tasting, check for allergies within the class.

Guy Fawkes Night (UK)

Guy Fawkes Night or Bonfire Night is celebrated each year on 5 November. On this date in 1605 Guy Fawkes tried to blow up the British Parliament and the unpopular King James I. Many hated him as he introduced harsh laws against the Catholics. The plot to blow up the king and his parliament was led by Robert Catesby but Guy Fawkes was the one chosen to light the gunpowder. The conspirators were caught and later executed. On the 5 November people make bonfires on which a figure, or 'guy', made from old clothes stuffed with straw or paper is burned. The purpose is to remember the conspirators and their bid for religious tolerance. The celebration includes displays of fireworks and feasts of bonfire toffee, hot dogs and jacket potatoes.

Monet Houses of Parliament

Claude Monet (1840–1926) was a French Impressionist who painted a series of paintings of the Houses of Parliament (1900–1904) during his stay in London. They were all painted from the same viewpoint, Monet's window at St Thomas' Hospital looking out over the river Thames, but at different times of the day and during different weather and light conditions.

Resources

- Pictures of Monet's *Houses of Parliament, London*
- Cartridge paper
- Chalk pastels
- Pictures of the Houses of Parliament

Approach

1 Show the children copies of Monet's *Houses of Parliament, London.* Explain that this was the building Guy Fawkes intended to blow up in 1605 almost 300 years before Monet painted these pictures.

2 Discuss how the light changes and transforms the image of the building. Ask the children if they can identify the time of day, season and weather conditions when each picture was painted. Talk about the colours Monet used.

3 Give the children a piece of cartridge paper and chalk pastels.

4 Cut out pictures, postcards or draw pictures of the Houses of Parliament and stick onto the cartridge paper.

5 Ask the children to choose a mood of sky they want to create. Use chalk pastels to colour the sky.

Bonfire Display

Resources

- Large flame-shaped pieces of fabric stuck onto card
- Collage materials, e.g. sequins, wool
- Coloured pipe cleaners
- Paint and brushes
- Scissors and glue

Approach

1 Explain to the children that on 5 November people light bonfires and burn a 'guy'. There are parties with fireworks and special food. Tell the story of Guy Fawkes and the gunpowder plot.
2 Make large flames out of yellow, red and orange fabric. Give each child a flame to decorate with pictures of fireworks using collage material, sequins etc.
3 Display as a large bonfire.

Cross-curricular Links

- **History** – Study the reign of James I. Make a timeline of events that led to the gunpowder plot.
- **PSHCE** – Discuss the dangers of Bonfire Night and make a poster of sensible rules to follow, such as never go near or back to a firework that has been lit and only adults should light fireworks.

Dreidel Template

- Make a copy of this template and cut it out from some cardboard (for example, a cereal box).
- Decorate the template before folding it into shape (see page 8 for information on the traditional designs).
- Make a small hole in the circle that is big enough for a wooden skewer to pass through.
- Fold and glue the template into the Dreidel shape (see examples on page 8).
- Push a wooden skewer through the hole and secure it with Sellotape®.

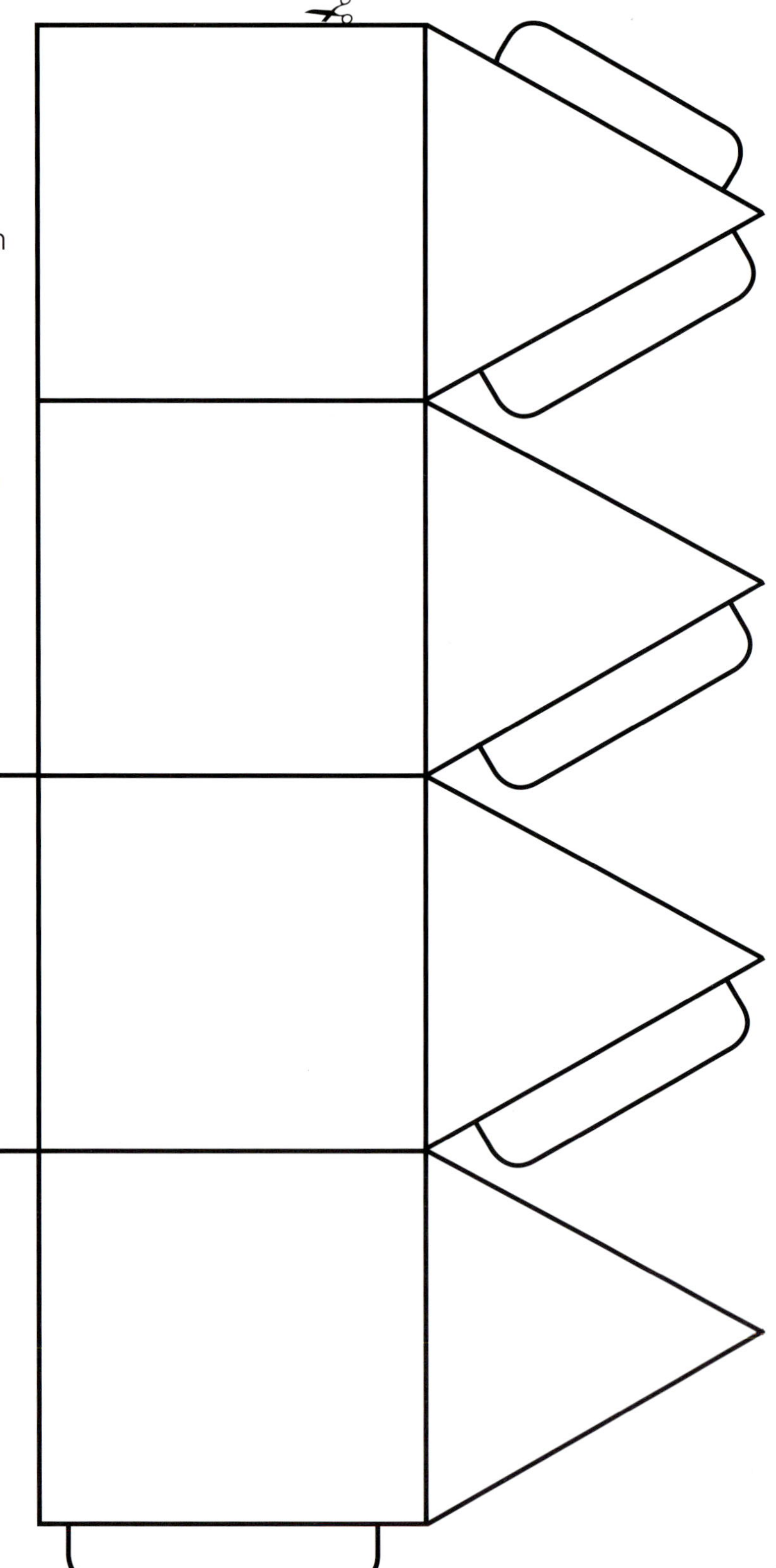